MONTVILLE TWP. PUBLIC LIBRARY
90 HORSENECK ROAD
MONTVILLE, NJ 07045

J 595.79
Twist
Twist, Clint

The Life Cycle of Honey Bees

Montville Township Public Library
90 Horseneck Road
Montville, N.J. 07045-9626
973-402-0900
Library Hours

Monday	9 a.m.-9 p.m.
Tuesday	9 a.m.-9 p.m.
Wednesday	9 a.m.-9 p.m.
Thursday	9 a.m.-9 p.m.
Friday	9 a.m.-6 p.m.
Saturday	9 a.m.-5 p.m.
Sunday	12 p.m.-5 p.m.

see website www.montvillelibrary.org

The Life Cycle of Honey Bees

An Hachette Company

First published in the United States by
New Forest Press, an imprint of Octopus Publishing Group Ltd

www.octopusbook.usa.com

Copyright © Octopus Publishing Group Ltd 2012

Published by arrangement with Black Rabbit Books
PO Box 784, Mankato, MN 56002

All rights reserved. No part of this work may be reproduced or utilized in any form or by any means, electronic or mechanical, including photocopying, recording or by any information storage and retrieval system, without the prior written permission of the publisher.

Library of Congress Cataloging-in-Publication Data

Twist, Clint.
The Life Cycle of Honey Bees / by Clint Twist.
p. cm. -- (Creepy crawlies)
Includes index.
Summary: "Describes the life of a honeybee by explaining its body parts, habitat, and behaviors. Explains how the honeybees care for their hive, work together, and collect nectar to make honey. Compares the honeybee to other bees and insects. Includes life-cycle diagram and close-up photos of body parts"--Provided by publisher.
ISBN 978-1-84898-516-2 (hardcover, library bound)
1. Honey bee--Life cycles--Juvenile literature. I. Title.
QL568.A6T856 2013
595.79'9--dc23
2012003598

Printed and bound in the USA

16 15 14 13 12 1 2 3 4 5

Publisher: Tim Cook Editor: Margaret Parrish Designer: Steve West

Picture credits:
b=bottom; c=center; t=top; r=right; l=left
FLPA Images: 2-3, 8-9c, 11 all, 30c. Science Photo Library: 15r, 17t, 18-19 all, 20b, 21t, 22, 23t.
Shutterstock: 9b. Ticktock Image Archive: 23b, 24-27 all, 29, 31.

Every effort has been made to trace the copyright holders, and we apologize in advance for any unintentional omissions. We would be pleased to insert the appropriate acknowledgments in any subsequent edition of this publication.

0 1021 0281104 3

Contents

What Are Honey Bees?

Honey bees are furry-looking, winged insects that produce honey. They make a distinctive buzzing sound when they fly and can deliver a painful sting.

Honey bees, together with yellow jackets, ants, and termites, are called social insects because they live in a giant family group called a colony. Most honey bees are workers that collect nectar and pollen from flowers.

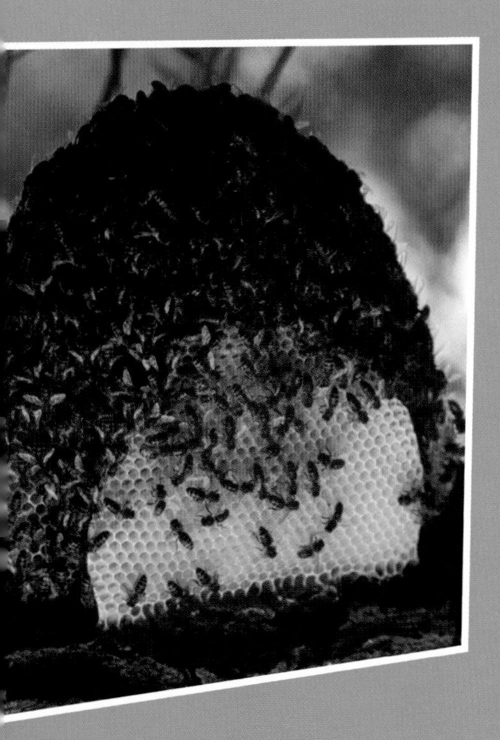

Honey bees live in hives.

Honey bees live where flowers are plentiful. They eat nectar and pollen from flowers and collect tree resin, which they use to make "bee glue." Bee glue is used to seal the hive. Honey bees have superb flight control and can hover in midair.

Who's Who?

Insects belong to a group of animal known as arthropods. Adult arthropods have jointed legs but no inner skeleton. Instead, they have a tough outer exoskeleton. All insects have six legs when they are adults, and most adult insects have wings and use either one pair or two pairs for flight.

Honey bees have two pairs of wings for flight.

Up Close and Personal

The honey bee worker is about 2/3 in (1.6 cm) long and has six legs and two pairs of wings for flight. It is divided into three parts—head, thorax, and abdomen.

A worker bee in flight

he abdomen is largest part
f the bee's body and contains
e digestive system. The head
as antennae, eyes, a brain,
nd a mouth. The thorax is
e middle part of the body; it
packed with muscles used
power the wings and legs.
oney bees have a special
rgan called the honey-stomach.
ectar is stored here.

Six Legs

Insects are sometimes called hexapods because they have six legs ("hex" means six in Latin). All insects are hexapods, but not all hexapods are insects. Springtails, for instance, have six legs but are not true insects.

Honeybees have six legs, like all other insects.

Hive Home

A honey bee colony is a huge family of bees. The bees build a nest called a hive, which is a busy, highly organized place.

Honey bees set up colonies in hollow trees. If trees are in short supply, the bees build hives under roofs, in old termite mounds, underground, or in caves.

The queen bee is the single fertile female in the colony. She never leaves the hive.

The colony includes about 300 male bees called drones. They are smaller than queens, but bigger than workers.

Most of the other honey bees (about 50,000 per colony) are workers (infertile females).

Home, Sweet Hive

A hive is not just a home. It contains everything the colony needs to survive, including the queen bee, the developing larvae, and the colony's food supply. To protect the hive, worker bees cover their nests in propolis, which they make from tree resin.

A honey-bee hive

Queen Bees

Queen bees are the largest honey bees—about 1 in (2.5 cm) long. A queen makes several mating flights early in life. During a mating flight, she is fertilized by drones from nearby hives. She then establishes a new colony.

Fed and cared for by worker bees, the queen lays thousands of eggs a day for the rest of her life. The queen controls how the eggs develop. Most become worker bees because the colony always needs workers. Workers live for about five weeks.

A queen bee inspects a cell in her hive

The queen occasionally lays eggs that hatch into drones. She will only lay "queen eggs" when the colony needs a new queen.

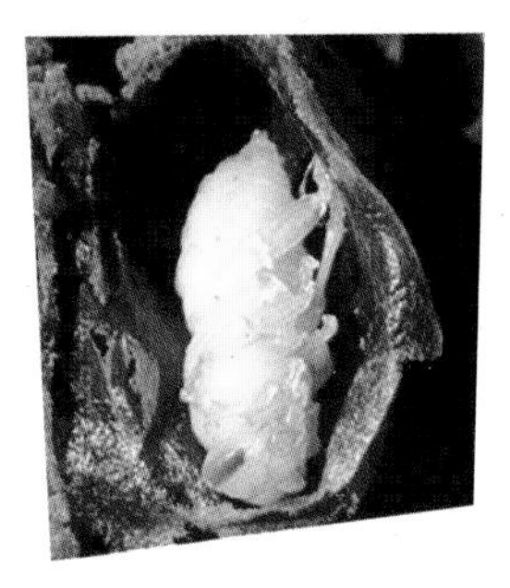

Pupa of a queen bee

Killer Queens

When it is time for a new queen, the old queen lays several queen eggs at once. All the eggs receive the same care, and the first to emerge becomes the next queen. The first act of a new queen is to sting to death all the other potential queens.

Worker honey bees surround a queen honey bee (marked with a pink dot). There is just one queen in a hive.

Cells of Life

The hive is a marvelous example of insect architecture. The queen lays eggs into individual cells made of beeswax.

Workers build and maintain the cells.

Each cell has six sides that fit closely together. After an egg is laid, workers seal the cell with wax.

Inside the cell, the egg hatches into a larva. The larva is the juvenile (young) form of a bee. The larvae are fed by workers that uncap the cells, feed them pollen and honey, and reseal the cells.

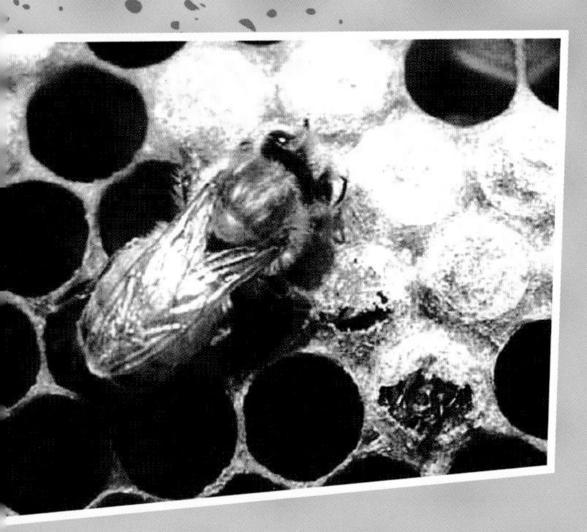

Young bees emerging

Inside the pupal case the larva transforms into an adult, a process known as metamorphosis. After a few days or a few weeks, a fully formed young bee emerges.

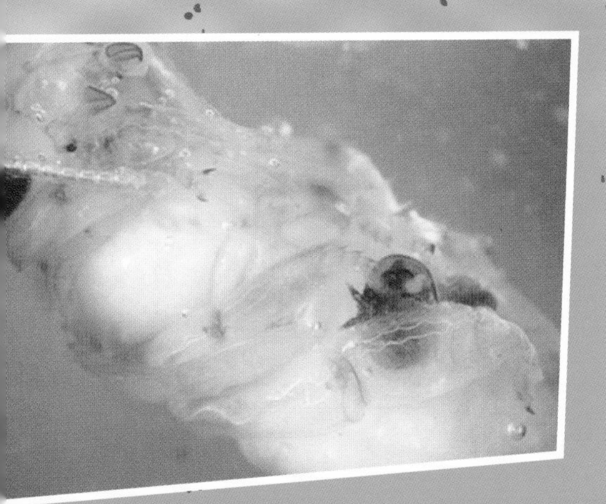

Close-up of a bee pupa

Development

Insects develop from eggs in two ways. With many insects, including bees, the eggs hatch into larvae that look different from the adults. The larvae go through a stage called metamorphosis, when they change into adults. With other kinds of insect, such as cockroaches and grasshoppers, the eggs hatch into nymphs that have adult body shapes.

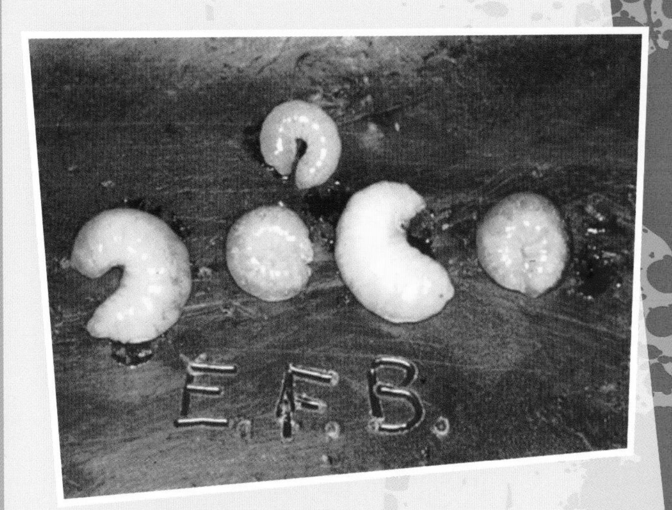

European honey bee larvae

Repairs and Guard Duty

After a worker bee emerges from its cell, it spends about three weeks inside the hive. At first, its duties keep it among the cells.

Cells must be kept in good condition and ready for new eggs.

Young workers repair the cells and make new ones. Workers produce wax in glands on the sides of their abdomens. They use their mouths to press the wax in place.

The head of a worker bee

The youngsters then progress to guard duty. Their job is to keep out intruders. They also flutter their wings at the entrance of the hive to create air currents that cool the hive.

Guard bees will kill an intruder to the hive.

Ultimate Sacrifice

A worker bee's stinger contains barbs that hold it firmly in its victim's flesh while poison is injected. When the bee pulls away, the stinger is torn out of its abdomen and left behind. The unfortunate bee dies soon afterward.

A bee's stinger

Finding Flowers

Honey bees really love flowers because they produce pollen and nectar. Flowering plants must really like honey bees, too, because they do their best to attract them.

Flowers produce pollen so that one flower can fertilize another of the same species. Honey bees help plants by carrying pollen from flower to flower.

Grains of pollen get lodged among the hairs of the bees' bodies. These are spread to other flowers, resulting in a process called pollination.

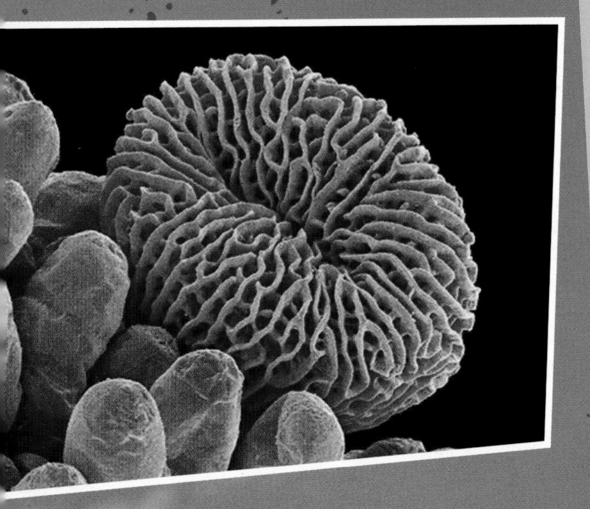

Close-up of pollen grain

Bees have excellent eyesight. They can see in color and in UV color as well. Flower petals have patterns that attract honey bees but are invisible to humans.

A daisy in UV light

Sweet Tooth

Many plants produce sweet, sugary nectar. This high-energy food is a favorite meal of honey bees.

Honeybees are attracted to flowers because of their nectar and pollen.

Waggle Dance

Each morning that plants are in flower, scout bees head out to find sources of pollen and nectar. Scouts are usually older, more experienced workers.

The scout bees fly up to 2 miles (3 km) in all directions during their search. When a scout returns to the hive it reports what it has found using the waggle dance.

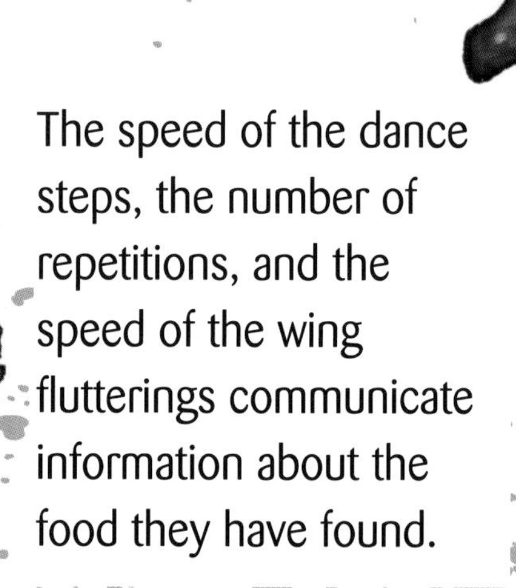

The speed of the dance steps, the number of repetitions, and the speed of the wing flutterings communicate information about the food they have found.

Scouts perform a figure-eight dance; the path of the dance indicates the way to the food.

Navigation

Honey bees navigate (find their way around) by using the Sun. The bees can judge where they are based on the direction of the Sun, the height of the Sun in the sky, and the strength of sunlight.

The Sun is the bees' navigation system.

Busy Bees

For the rest of their short lives, worker bees collect pollen and nectar every day to feed the hive.

Workers gather pollen with their mouths and front legs and carry it back to the hive in pollen baskets on their back legs. Nectar is carried inside a worker's honey-stomach.

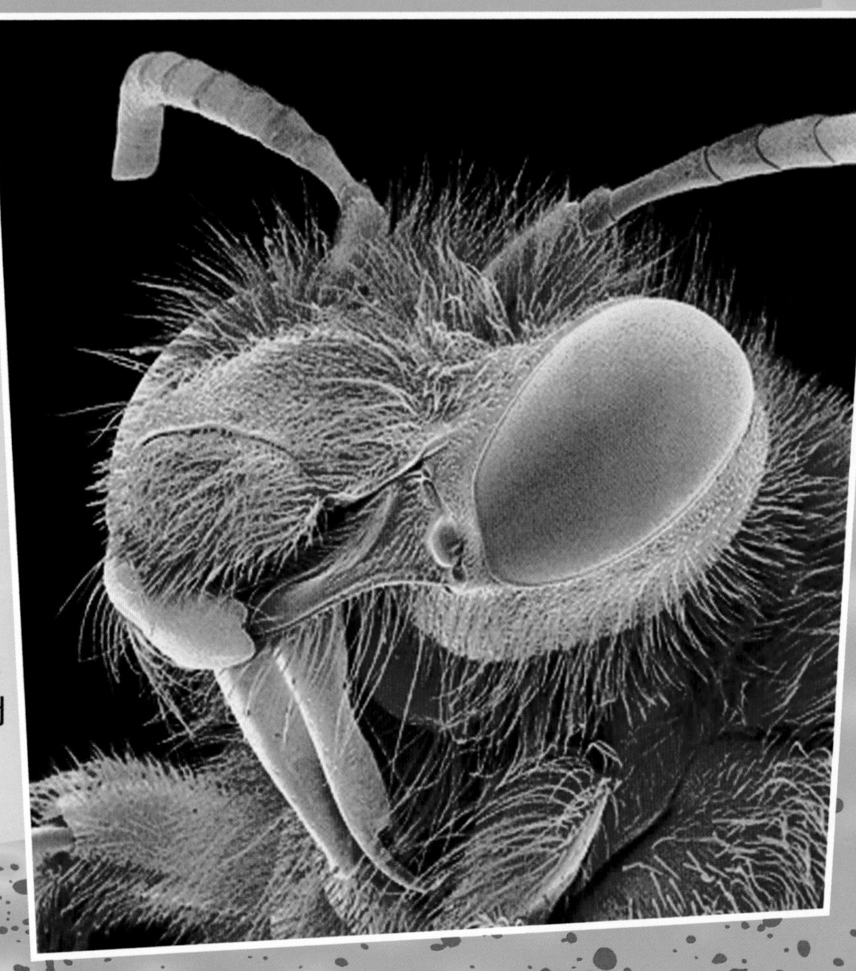

A worker bee's mouthparts

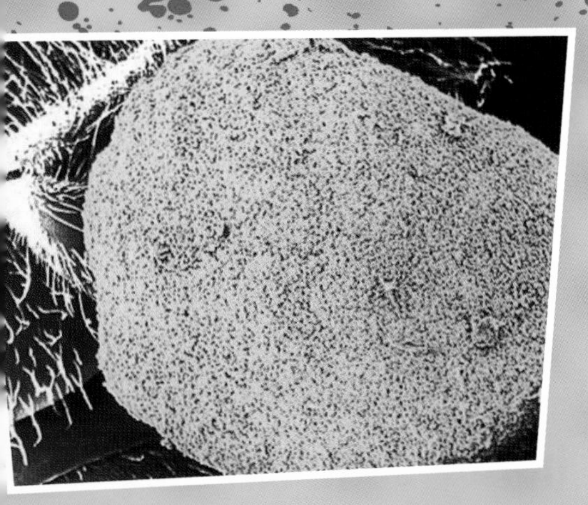

A pollen basket

Food that is not consumed immediately is stored in empty egg cells that have been cleaned and resealed.

Resin from trees is made into propolis, which is vital for good hive hygiene.

Honey bees collect water—which all animals need—and tree resin, which they turn into propolis, or "bee glue," used to seal the hive.

Honeycombs

Honey is made from regurgitated nectar and stored in honey cells. The close-fitting honey cells are called a honeycomb. The word honeycomb also describes any arrangement of closely packed, straight-sided hollow cells.

A honeycomb has hexagonal cells.

Honey Bees and Humans

Many animals enjoy the taste of honey, and some even eat bees. Humans like honey so much that we turned honey bees into farm animals over 5,000 years ago.

A bee colony can be a man-made hive constructed from mud, straw, or wood. If the colony is fed when there is no pollen or nectar naturally available, the stored honey can be removed and the bees will survive.

Beekeepers inspecting colonies

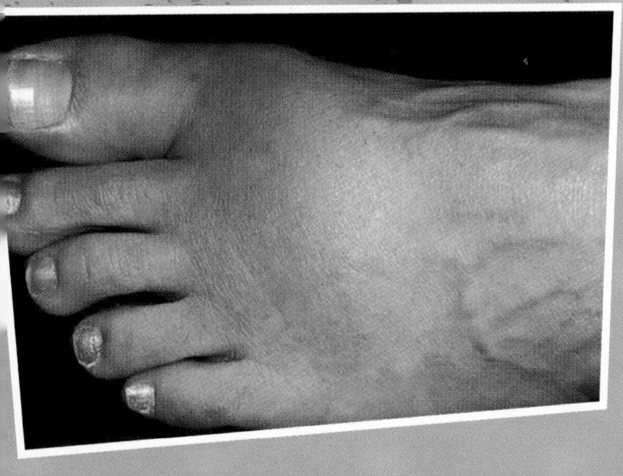

Bee venom injected during an attack causes redness, pain, swelling, and itching.

Each bee sting contains a small amount of mild poison, and only a few people are badly affected by a single sting. Lots of stings can be harmful, however, so beekeepers wear protective clothing.

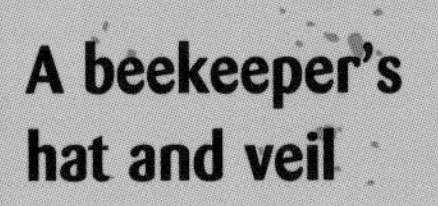

A beekeeper's hat and veil

Candlelight

For thousands of years, candles were made from beeswax, which burns brightly and has a pleasant smell. Other materials are now commonly used in candlemaking, but even today the best quality candles are made of beeswax.

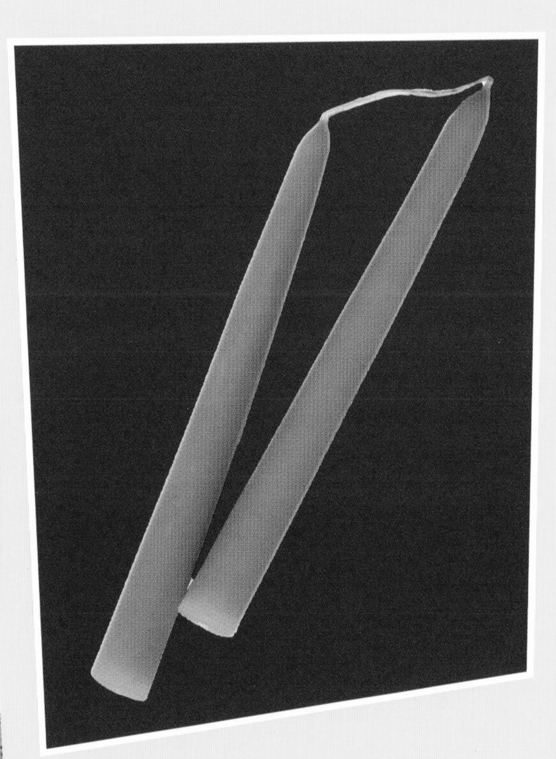

Candles made of genuine beeswax

Different Bees

Most bees have a different lifestyle than honey bees. Some live in small colonies, and some are solitary. Most eat nectar and pollen, but none builds up such big stockpiles of honey. There are about 20,000 species of bee.

Bumblebees

Bumblebees are bigger, hairier, and noisier than honey bees. They have typical warning colors: black and yellow or black and red. They live in far smaller colonies with a queen and 20 to 200 family members. Bumblebees are able to sting more than once and survive. Only the queen lives through the winter. She does this by hibernating in a burrow.

Carpenter Bees

Female carpenter bees use their mandibles (mouthparts) to chisel out holes in dead wood. At the bottom of each hole the bee lays a few eggs. Even a single carpenter bee can do a lot of damage to a piece of wooden furniture.

Cuckoo bees

These solitary bees are parasites on other bees. Like cuckoo birds, cuckoo bees do not build their own nests. Instead, female cuckoo bees invade the nests of other solitary bees. The cuckoo larvae eat the host's eggs.

Leafcutter bees

Leafcutter bees are solitary bees—they live alone. They use their powerful jaws to tunnel into soil and to cut leaves. The leaves are rolled into tubes and inserted into the tunnel. An egg is laid in this "leaf cell" before it is sealed up with a supply of pollen and nectar.

Bee Mimics

Identifying different bees can be difficult, because many insects look like bees—often so they can get inside a hive without being stung by guard bees. They are called bee mimics.

Drone fly

The drone fly belongs to a group of flying insect known as hover flies, many of which are bee or wasp mimics. The drone fly looks like a honey bee drone. It feeds from flowers in the open sunshine.

Greater bee fly

The greater bee fly looks like some bee species, except that is has a long mouthpart called a proboscis. It uses its proboscis to feed on nectar. Females lay their eggs close to solitary bee burrows. The fly larvae invade the burrows and eat the bee larvae.

Velvet ant

Despite its name, the velvet ant is a wasp. It is an even more aggressive parasite than the cuckoo bee. The female enters a nest and lays her eggs near a mature larva or a pupa. The velvet ant larvae then attacks it.

Bumble fly

The bumble fly is a hover fly that looks similar to a real bumblebee (shown in the photo). The bumble fly has no stinger, but its appearance offers it some protection from predators. It feeds on nectar and pollen.

Find Out More

Life Cycle

There are three types of honey bee inside each colony, each with a specific purpose. Queens produce eggs; drones or males mate with a queen from another colony; while workers—sterile females—bring back food. Once an egg hatches into a larva, the type of adult it develops into is determined by what type of food it is fed. A colony has just one queen bee. The life cycle of a honey bee is illustrated in the diagram below.

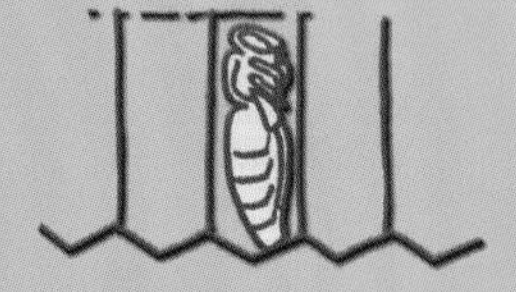

5b. Larvae fed with royal jelly produce males (drones) and females (queens). A new queen either kills the existing queen or forms a new colony by swarming (taking some of the workers with her).

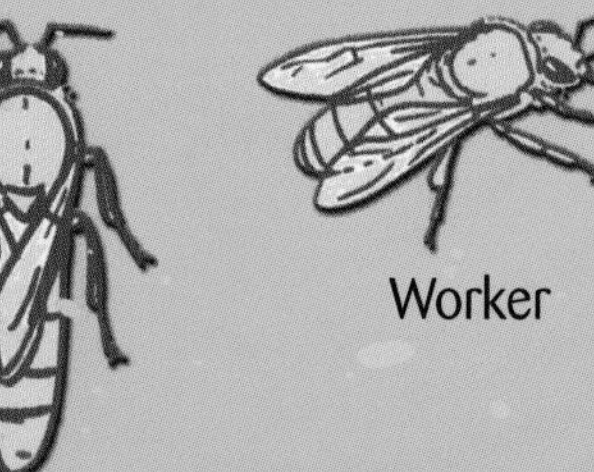

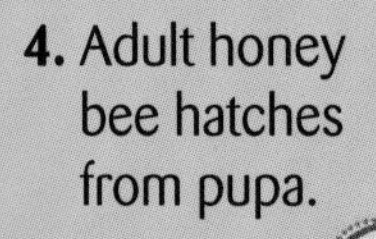

5a. Most adults are sterile females (workers) that clean the nest, look after the larvae, and collect nectar and pollen.

Fabulous Facts

Fact 1: There are about 20,000 species of bee, but only about six are true honey bees.

Fact 2: Honey bees have been used by people since the age of the pyramids, around 5,000 years ago.

Fact 3: Honey bees originated in Tropical Africa and spread from South Africa to Northern Europe and East into India and China.

Fact 4: Fossilized bees date back 40 million years and are nearly identical to modern bees.

Fact 5: Each honey bee colony can contain tens of thousands of bees. Some colonies contain as many as 80,000 bees.

Fact 6: Larvae hatch from eggs in three to four days and are fed by worker bees.

Fact 7: A queen lives three to five years; drones usually die by winter; workers live for about five weeks.

Fact 8: A queen is fed a high-protein food produced by young workers that enables her to lay up to 2,000 eggs a day. This is about twice her own weight.

Fact 9: A queen makes several mating flights during her life. She stores the sperm from up to 20 drones that she collects on those flights. Drones that mate with her die in the act.

Fact 10: Bees eat pollen to produce bee milk, sometimes called royal jelly. They feed this to the queen continuously and to larvae for three days after they hatch from eggs.

Fact 11: To make 2 lb (1 kg) of wax, a bee has to eat about 9 lb (4 kg) of honey. They secrete wax scales from four pairs of glands under their abdomens.

Fact 12: The scientist Karl von Frisch studied the behavior of honey bees and was awarded the Nobel Prize for physiology and medicine in 1973. Von Frisch noticed that honey bees communicate with the language of dance.

Fact 13: Drone bees, which are larger than worker bees, have no stingers. The queen bee has a smooth stinger and could sting multiple times, but the queen does not leave the hive under normal conditions.

Glossary

Abdomen—the largest part of an insect's three-part body; the abdomen contains many important organs.

Antennae—a pair of special sense organs found at the front of the head on most insects.

Arthropod—any creepy crawly that has jointed legs; insects and spiders are arthropods.

Beeswax—a sticky, solid substance produced by honey bees and used for building cells.

Cell—a hollow, six-sided structure made by honey bees and used for raising young and storing honey.

Colony—a group of insect, or other living thing, that lives very closely together.

Digestive system—the organs that are used to process food.

Drone—a male honey bee; drones are larger than workers but cannot sting.

Exoskeleton—a hard outer covering that protects and supports the bodies of some animals.

Gland—a part of an animal's body that produces particular substances.

Hive—the nest made by a colony of honey bees.

Honey—sweet, syrupy substance produced by honey bees. It is made from nectar, although it usually includes some pollen.

Honeycomb—a collection of cells built side-by-side inside a hive.

Insect—a kind of creepy crawly that has six legs; most insects also have wings.

Jaws—hinged structures around the mouth that allow some animals to bite and chew.

Larva—a wormlike creature that is the juvenile (young) stage in the life cycle of many insects.

Nectar—a sweet, sugary substance produced by flowering plants and used by honey bees to make honey.

Nymph—the juvenile (young) stage in the life cycle of insects that do not produce larvae.

Organ—a part of an animal's body that performs a particular task; for instance, the heart pumps blood.

Parasite—any living thing that lives or feeds on or in the body of another living thing.

Pollen—tiny, multisided grains that are produced by flowers to fertilize other flowers of the same species.

Pupa—the pupa represents the stage in the life cycle of some insects in which the body of a mature larva is transformed into an adult insect.

Pupation—the process by which insect larvae change their body shape to the adult form.

Queen—the largest honey bee in a colony; the queen is the only bee in the hive that can lay eggs.

Skeleton—an internal structure of bones that supports the bodies of large animals such as mammals, reptiles, and fish.

Thorax—the middle part of an insect's body where the wings and legs are attached. The thorax is packed with muscles.

UV—ultraviolet light that cannot be detected by human eyes, but is seen by honey bees.

Waggle dance—a pattern of movements used by honey bees to communicate the direction, distance, and nature of food sources.

Worker—a sterile female honey bee; nearly all the honey bees in a hive are workers.

Index

MONTVILLE TWP. PUBLIC LIBRARY
90 HORSENECK ROAD
MONTVILLE, N[illegible]45